Nonno,
My grief and gratitude dance harmoniously in the garden we walked through.
Where you taught me lessons, instilled unyielding strength,
power and determination into me.

You mastered the art of weaving wisdom into seemingly simplistic moments.
You are the one I measure all against, including myself.
My father figure, my champion, my greatest teacher,
your words echo in my soul and live on in my bones.

You showed me that anything is possible if you work hard enough,
that giving up is not an option and that you must carve your own path,
in business, in life and in love.

It was my honour to be your student, my honour to know you,
to love you, to forever admire you and as grief tears my heart apart,
gratitude sews it back together.
Your words and love gently lay all the pieces back into place.

I am forever grateful to have had you here, you are in my heart
and by my side always.

Now, as with all our conversations, I know you would end this
with a wink, a smile and of course, a capish.

Nonno, this is for you, ciao x

I write in the hope my words penetrate your soul.
That they may reach out across the chasm and
pull you into the light.
In the hope they make you feel a little more understood,
a little less alone and a lot more liberated
to live your truth, authentically, unapologetically and completely.
This book is a collection of the utterings of my soul,
made up of miniture moments, beautiful memories
and soul shifting lessons woven together to form
the incredible tapestry of what it is to be human.

Love, always, in all ways.

Ranxx

Metanoia;
The journey of changing ones mind, heart, self or way of life; A spiritual conversion.
For there are many things I used to be
That I am no longer and many things
I never thought I'd be that I unexpectedly am.
Therein lies the beauty of life.
The thousand skins we've shed and the thousand we are yet to wear.

To write is to have a love affair with language.
To fall deep and hard every day,
with spontaneity and reckless abandon.
To be transported to balconies in Paris
and mountains in Scotland.
To see into the heart of life, to connect,
To feel and tell the stories of our souls.
To live authentically, unapologetically and completely.
This is why I write;
in the hope that my words resonate,
make you feel a little more understood,
a little less alone and a lot more liberated to live your truth.
The world needs a little more truth.

We each carry a million stories,

That's how we teach and how we learn,

by sharing our stories.

we are all just one big tribe sitting around a fire

listening to our elders speak of life.

Maybe poets are
modern-day healers
putting bandaids on knees
and kissing scars.
maybe poems are
our kind looks
and gentle hand squeezes
reassuring the world
that we are not alone

We are the modern-day prophets,
standing on old milk crates,
yelling tales of love into the streets.

"What a funny thing life is"
She pondered as she walked home,
intrigued by her time here, her human experience.
"I shall not waste it" she thought.
"I shall throw myself in, relish it, because, as with all things,
It will be over just as I start to forget I don't live forever."

Poets are made after midnight, when the words come out to play amidst the memories and the melancholy.

Jan 21, 2020

2am Piano & Pinot

I waltz between chasing the tranquility of the mountains and the chaos of the storm if not to feel alive just for a moment.

To awaken the soul is to witness pure magic.

The alchemy of humans.

You will find you can forge a crown out of almost any debris.

She doesn't need protection,

She has her own shield.

She doesn't ask for help or the answers,

She comes to her own conclusions.

She doesn't need you to show her the way,

She carves her own path.

She doesn't need you to defend her

For she conjured the elements to bend for her.

She doesn't need you,

For she is a goddess of **Herculean Ferocity**

ADVERSITY IS NOT A KILLSHOT.

We are beautifully battle-hardened, my darling.

Poetry gives context to the painful joy of life.

It crosses centuries, cultures, languages and religions.

It's a light in the dark, a sanctuary of understanding.

Soup for the soul, LSD for the mind and love for the heart.

A home for weary heads, full pens and eager fingers,

My solace in solitude, the safety for my soul.

Forever the place my spirit comes home too.

She was born of grace and valour.
A queen amongst mortals
Pure of heart with fire in her bones
She can warm your soul and
set your world alight

She is both calm and storm;
Wolf and woman.
She is undefinable.
A paradox of gentle ferocity;
She is wild at heart and
shall not be tamed,

For that is part of her beauty,
The way she can make the madness
feel like a dance.
The alchemy of her;
it is something to behold.

Born of grace and valour;
A queen to love and go to war beside.
A queen we searched for in
our storybooks as young girls.

A queen who slayed dragons,
who fanned our flames,
who needed no knight
for she wielded her own sword.

Take a moment to appreciate her.
Women like her are a rare eclipse.
it is an honour to know her.
To run next to her,
to bathe in her sunlight.
An honour for the chosen few.

To Love her, to leave her wild.

2am disarms me like a French Poet with a bottle of single malt.

Whiskey, cigarettes and solitude;
That was her Poetry.

I have come to find there
are few dilemmas a dram of whiskey
and a tranquil moment cannot solve.

Her lovers are knowledge and nostalgia
and she dances between the aisles in the intoxicating aura
of her favourite books; a treasure trove for a curious mind.

Parents;
The empathy comes when you realize they're just like us.

Calling from beyond the grave, I just want to say hi dad.
I can't remember what it felt like to hold your hand, did I ever?
A little girl in big shoes trying to walk in your footsteps.
Oil on her small hands as she played with your tools,
her brow furrowed; determined to fix things.

Following you into the garden to mow the lawn on a hot summers' day,
pulling her t-shirt off because she wanted to be just like you.
Falling asleep on the couch next to you, cuddling her teddy.
Watching you refill your cup with red wine at 3pm, your eyes heavy.
Seeing you sway, even when the music wasn't playing,
you were always doing that.
You would pour another drink, then another;
it became a daily routine, your comfort or survival I suppose.

What monsters were you trying to drown?

I was a girl standing in front of a monster.
No oil on my hands, no footsteps to follow,
my brow still furrowed, from disappointment and confusion;
Where is my dad?

In a drunken stupor, a coward lay in front of me.
I didn't want to be like him anymore.
Bedtime stories were now fights of anger with
words of vitriol punctuated by slamming doors.
Tears of hatred turned to defeat
when I turned away where no one could see.

Sprawled on the floor,
the melancholy words poured through my pen
onto the tear-stained sheets of my notebook,
cigarette smoke danced on my lips.

I yearned for an honest moment;
As we pass each other as awkward strangers in the same kitchen,
I tell him 'You're an alcoholic" and with the same tired eyes
he responds "Yes, I hide in the bottle."
A daughter shouldn't yearn for a moment like that.

When all love is lost and there is nothing left to fight for,
honesty is all you have.
You were the monster I could never fight off.
I don't hate you, I don't love you.
at best you could say I'm not mad.
You taught me so much, not through encouraging words
or loving arms, no, through pain,
through fear and the feeling etched so deeply into my bones:
being truly ashamed of you; my father.
A daughter never forgets that.

I don't know you, I forgave you.
We are strangers now, maybe we always were.
I have hope for the future,
That the legacy of your mistakes,
your weakness, shall never be replicated by the ones you hurt.

His-Story shall never be repeated.

Where does all the love go when it's gone?

love

I think it floats around us in the air like Autumn leaves, ready to fall at anothers' feet.

Hold your head up, little girl,
turn your face toward the sun,
feel the warmth in your bones.
Walk forward into this life,
one earth cracking step at a time.

You will stumble, you will fall
but you will rise, again and again.
You will cast spells upon this world,
leaving magical glitter dust along the path you carve,
to light the way for the young queens that follow.

You see, this is our duty, my love.
To wield our gentle ferocity,
to break barriers, open doors,
to create magic with fire, love and kindness.

We grow wings,
and as we fly higher and higher,
the strength of our wind fans the flames of young queens.
We must never let our fire extinguish,
never let our childlike curiosity be quashed.

It is up to us to protect our wild;
let it thunder,
let it roar,
let it always wander freely.

That is our honour, our duty,
our greatest achievement,
and soon, my darling, it will be yours.

It was her unwavering faith in things,
her calm smile and knowing glance,
like she was in on a secret
that we would never know.

There it was,
In the middle of a village in Greece,
between the hum of simple life and the
sweetness of melting ice-cream,
a stirring reminder from the universe
delivered so masterfully on the T-shirt
of a young queen;
Where there is love, there is life.

Opening old dusty doors in the back of my mind.
I've left them behind,
Left them dormant,
in the hope that the monsters
lurking within found other children to scare.
Hiding under beds and in dark corners,
I startle at the shadows.
A little girl walking her own yellow brick road
"if only I had the courage of a lion" she whispered.

Words my nonno told me...

Words my Nonno told me;
She chases shadows down pathways,
meets demons with kind faces; they irk her.
Just when she feels she may succumb
to their seductive but insecure whispers,
she steels herself with his words;
"Remember the stories of feeble men
who come to steal your power in the night.

Who come on horseback with strong arms,
and speak of forever; of endless possibilities.
Who will trick you into trading parts of yourself
for the promise of love.
Until one day, you barely recognise
the woman staring back at you in the
reflection of the cage you didn't even realise you were in."

He told me they would come,
he told me they'd be trouble. "Be strong" he said
"Carry your head high and your stick over your shoulder.
They'll come for you, they won't be able to help themselves,
for they are boys wearing a mans mask,
And you are a formidable woman who needs no one.

Ride free, on your own,
never slow down.
Only those fast enough to keep up belong beside you.
Ride fast, ride free, as you need no one."

The sunday lunch table:
a place where past and present collide
over a full stomach and a glass of Cinzano
I listen to the lessons gently woven
into stories of the old country.
Maybe it's the Cizano fog
or the distant sound of Sinatra
on the record player that makes
his eyes dance, maybe it's sharing
fond memories with his granddaughter.
To me it's a glimmer of magic.

To me, this is where peace is found; in the quiet moment between turning pages and pouring coffee.

*And if I am ever lost,
you may find me nestled in a nook,
surrounded by the dog-eared pages
of my favourite books,
with the steam of hot, black coffee
and inked words dancing in the air.
You may find me there.
You may find me
where the wild words are.*

Home,
Where the smell of coffee and freshly
baked scones dances in the air.
Where laughter bounces off the walls
and lands on your soul.

Home, where the hugs are the best
and the only remedy for any type of day.
Where the food tastes better and
has a way of filling your heart and your stomach.
Where stillness can be sourced at any moment.

Where the garden is a beautiful sanctuary
and the flowers seem to whisper as I walk past.

Where love is always found.
Where mum is a verb, noun,
adjective and religion.

Home, I carry you in my heart always
and when I leave, I hide a piece of me
somewhere for safekeeping until I return.

Mum,

1979

Dogs; The Original Stoics.

I have never searched for love,
I have always known just where to find it;
At my feet, looking up,
with deep golden eyes
and a wagging tail.
How honoured we are
to have the love of dogs.

The blank page;
A daunting prospect or a merciful release
for the words dancing around my head.
It depends on the day.
See thats the beauty of the blank page,
like young love, she keeps me guessing.
Every day is different and I am forever
torn between the dichotomy
of excitement and anxiety.
Maybe that's what keeps me coming back,
night after night, pen in hand,
eternally searching for the words
to describe the excrutiating
yet addictive draw of her;
The blank page.

It was December,
3am on a Tuesday,
She was half a bottle in.
The Shiraz dancing on her tongue.
She was tired, restless, sleepless
stuck in the limbo; the inbetween
of what has passed and what will be.
The relentless Groundhog Day.

And so,

I arrive at this page a little tired,

a few months older, and always, with a whiskey in hand.

The truth of it is, we live, we love, we fall, we repair.

Therein lies the fabric of life.

I take stock of it all. I breathe in,

smell the cold, sweet, Autumn air,

the taste of peated whiskey on my tongue.

That deep sense of self always waiting for me in the wings,

ready for me to slide over my shoulders

like a favourite winter coat as the seasons subtly change.

It is never lost, never broken.

never too far away, like a distant island off the coast

I return home after months at sea;

To Myself, For Myself, By Myself.

There is no emptiness,

just more room to flourish.

Meanwhile, on a hot Summers' night, somewhere deep in the heart of Barcelona, A girl discovers a love for old vinyls, new friends and strong cigars.

Maybe;
Maybe it's a little more you and a little less them.
Maybe it's more vibe and less words.
Maybe it's more get your mind right,
keep your hustle tight, focus on your own light.
Maybe it's running your own race,
not sweating the pace or losing face.
Maybe it's a little more protecting your wild,
loving the plot twists and listening to your inner child.

There is nothing to be afraid of, my love.
Stepping into yourself is always the right move.
Having the honest conversation is always the right answer.
You know, she knows, your gut knows, your soul knows;
down to the tips of your fingers - you know.
Hold yourself in grace and power,
Speak with gentle strength and a loving will.
Whisper your kind truth;
The universe will listen, she always does.

Days of black coffee, nights of red wine and all th while, words are running through my head like they're late for the train..

And she sat, looking out into the darkness

The distant rumble of the ocean,

the score of her moment.

Breathing in the crisp air,

smoke dancing around her.

The fog of whiskey bringing that heavy-eyed,

satisfied smile to her face.

She loved it, you know,

Those private moments

when she dove into her vices.

After all, don't we all become

philosophers with a whiskey in one

hand and a cigarette in the other?

July 14th

*Poetry comes at night,
amid the stars that seem to wink
after that second glass of wine.
Funny how the moonlight
makes poets out of us all.*

Unsubscribe;
From the emails, mailing lists
and mindless conversations.
From the time-wasters, the shit talkers,
the never going to 'walk the walk-ers'
From the ones who never listen but can't stop talking,
From the haters that pretend they don't creep
but always be gawking.
From the falsities, the fakers,
the never going to 'make it makers'.
From the imposters, the liars, the energy drainers.
From the chest beaters, the 'never had a goal' keepers,
the make-believe trainers.
The pseudo-friends,
the insecure and perpetually damaged men.
From the sins that aren't yours,
but, evidently, you pay for.
From the heartache, the mistake,
the chance you said you'd never take.
Unsubscribe, shed your skin
because there's no longer any room left within.

Swimming under the stars at midnight is almost always the answer; the question is irrelevant.

A wild soul that craves the peace of a mountain top at sunrise.

Hello Beautiful

Break yourself open,
show me your shards
see as they glisten in the light
you try to hide them from.
For you are beautiful,
my darling.
Always, in all ways.

The girl with the charcoal heart.
She broke off pieces
and drew her new life
on the shattered walls
of her world.

She tore down hell
and built a universe
behind it.

Because hell hath no fury
like a queen who
uses her pain to
paint visions of love.

The seduction of our vices.
Those solitary moments,
just for us,
when we crack the door
of our inner citadel
and breathe, just for a moment.

Let laughter be the score to your fondest memories.

The best poetry
lies in the arches
of a broken heart.

3am, March 19th

For all the self awareness,
wisdom and growth,
Sometimes we're just
heartbroken humans,
stumbling home, drunk at 2am

A lucid moment in a foggy dream...

Time passes so effortlessly.
Sometimes we stop,
catch ourselves in a moment;
they are rare,
few and far between.

Years pass,
memories are made.
I know they will come,
maybe stay for a time but then they will go,
as they are meant too.
Yes, I could be describing the moments that make up a lifetime,
you would not be blamed for thinking that.
But no, it is not the moments I mean this time,

It is those that will come before you,
those that yearn to find a home within me.
I will give them my time,
maybe let them in a slightly ajar door,
but they are not home to me.

They are stories I will tell,
memories I may remember,
but not my home.
You will have them too and we will speak of them fondly.
I will laugh,
you will smile and when you hold my face in your hand
it will feel like home and I will wonder
how I ever lived anywhere else.

It is essential to the
human experience
to get your heart broken
at least twice.

August 30, 2018

Don't look back.

The dichotomy of falling for the ideal, not the real.

Honesty; A letter.
Sometimes I've hated you in the moments of motivation
but I cannot lie; it motivated me.
There's a weird dynamic between us; with a hint of competition,
a lot of love and an odd, knowing connection that runs so deep,
I could never find words to explain it.
We drive each other without wanting to admit it.
It's the sometimes harsh truths that hit me hard because deep down,
I believe them too.
I've been saying them to myself but thought I was the only one who knew.
I thought I had hidden them so well from anyone else.
The truth is I find it refreshing to be held accountable.
That's the space where you actually have the chance to take action
because you're forced into the light, you're seen,
there's no hiding. It's scary and liberating.
The thought "Fuck, I'm seen, there's no going back now"
I've learned to love that.
I've learned to search for it in conversations.
I push it on others in the hope they'll reciprocate.
I do this because I know it will elevate me to the next level.
Force me, sometimes uncomfortably, into a different perspective.
I can't be mad at what you've said, it's the truth.
The delivery, devoid of tact, has been questionable at times
but then maybe the sharpness allowed for the cut through.
The fact that I can stand back, look at the person I am
and be really fucking happy, proud and fiercely driven is a wonderful thing
and there is no denying,you have been a part of that.
We've learnt from each other, we still do, that's important.
I don't know if it's commonplace in relationships but I do know it's special.
So thank you.For your honesty.For your care.
For your candor even when you were unsure of the response.

I don't care where it came from - love, insecurity, a desire to truly help,
A deep knowing of what I really needed.
I don't care. I used it, I use it still.
It's made me fiercer, kept me hungry,
it's forged me into a warrior.
Thank you,
no matter what.

Balconies were invented to scream secrets into the night with a wine-stained tongue.

It was that die for you, cry for you,
never tell a lie to you love,
That visceral, metaphysical,
completely inexplicable love.
That deep pain, do it in vain,
never leaves you the same love.

Over time, crossed every line,
partners in crime love.
That slow ache, of a heart break,
knowing it's a mistake type of love.

That "I know better" "I'll do better"
empty promises in your letter love.
That lonely when we're together,
days of stormy weather,
I'm hanging on by a tether love.

That broken, not a word spoken,
a closed door my only token of your love.
That ride or die, always flying high,
you'll forever be my guy love.

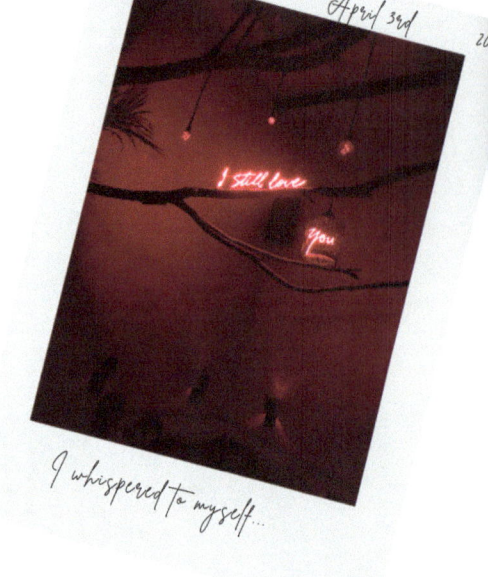

April 3rd

I whispered to myself...

I remember how the sheets felt,
how we moved in your bed.
I can taste the pages on your lips
of all the books you've read.

The Luxury of Ignorance.

The sweetness that dripped from your lips turned to acid on my skin.

Arms of safe embrace became a cage of posession.

Whispers of ownership lingered between your words.

I could taste them.

I could feel them creeping over me like claustrophobia.

You called it love,

you presented it like a beautiful necklace

that swiftly became a noose around my neck.

Chances of redemption given and squandered.

You spoke of things you did not understand,

used words from a language you didn't speak,

but you have something I do not;

The luxury of ignorence.

The big, hungry appetite of a heart

not yet broken and built back.

I think it's right for you to feel ashamed,

to stand by all the mistakes you made.

You've lost the stars from you eyes,

some hope from your heart, but my god,

I hope you gained a lesson.

If only to lose the luxury of ignorance.

A hand squeeze,
A slow tease, got that weakness in my knees.
A quick bite, she shows no fight,
She's mine, maybe only for the night.

It's lust, never discussed, spoken only through trust.
The smell of perfume on her skin, the shudder within
as she lets me sink in.

Watching her; eyes closed, losing her mind,
slowly on her grind, the way she moves is undefined.
It's damn real, tapping into those deep parts of feel,
you know, those ones we fight like hell to conceal.

But I am misaligned, and I come to find,
by morning, she's left me behind.
She tasted like sin and whiskey, sweet and risky,
her lingering kiss left me tipsy.

And what a taste it was, a delicious harlet,
the devil incarnate she devoured me,
and all thats left are my scars of scarlet.

You see she was worlds apart;
Because she had mastered the art,
Of the forehead kiss and the bite mark.

"It's her eyes" he said
"Th way they draw you in,
whisper to you in a language you've
never heard yet you speak it fluently.
They can change in a flash and envelop you."
"Her eyes" he said
"I feel if I ever lose their gaze,
I might cease to exist."

I know you loved me.
I know you did in your own way.
I know it was excruciating.
I know you tried hard, in spite of yourself.
Do you think of the night we met?
Do you wish it were all different?

That, if only a moment earlier, or a second later,
we may have remained strangers?
But it wasn't that way, it was exactly how it happened.

And so, let's not look upon it as a failure, as a journey of futile efforts,
No, let's look upon those years with settled souls and learned hearts.
Because in the end, it's all a matter of perspective isn't it?

Reaching into the hidden parts of each other's hearts,
stirring fractured souls, feeling so much we could barely catch our breath;
how could that ever be deemed a failure?
It is, by all accounts, the tapestry of our human experience.

Let's look upon those years with grateful hearts and warm smiles.
How lucky we were to taste the sweetness of young love,
the bitterness of pain, the saltiness of broken tears.

How lucky we were to succumb to the exquisite depth of love,
so deep we lost sight of the surface.
And now, it's time for you to breathe again.
To find the surface, breakthrough and breathe deep.

Because my love, the time has come to release me.
Release all of me and breathe again.
It's time to let go, it's time to breathe.

Be wary;

She draws in **charcoal**

but has the most

colourful mind.

Those dusk rays light up the road and bounce off your chevvy.
That 67 blue reminds me of the ocean,
We set the scene like Bonnie & Clyde;
our own public enemies.

My feet on the dash, your hands on the wheel.
My eyes peeking out from under my favourite Stetson hat,
drinking in your tanned skin glowing in the sun.
You catch my eye, our souls dancing with the thrill of it all.

Wild Spirits and Fast Cars
with the wind in our hair whispering secrets in my ear.
You slide your hand over my leg and on that highway,
somewhere in Nevada, between the past and a dream,
We lit the world alight and it was fucking beautiful.

It was that Summer love,
set against the golden hour.
If you look closely,
you can catch a glimpse of it,
nestled between a girls resting head
and a boys willing shoulder.
That Summer love that lasted a lifetime.

Love is a decision.
The choice is mine.
I choose me.
I choose you.
I choose us.

*Let's play truth or dare,
I dare you to play yourself,
truthfully.*

Because you move me.
Run wild with me.
Be yourself with me,
Surrender with me, Liberate me,
For those beautiful reasons,
I will always return to you.

The exquisite pain.

The ache of regret.

For all the years he'd had her within reach but dare not touch her

For all the moments she was in front of him with an open heart.

For all the nights she lay, cold, yearning for his touch

And for this moment;

The moment he realises he will never have her again.

Never feel her warm gaze

never be thawed by her unwavering love.

For those moments, he's filled with regret.

He tastes it on his tongue

He feels it in his bones and sees it reflected back at him

when he has the strength to look himself in the mirror.

It is a friend to him now.

Like a shadow, never too far behind him.

It's what he knows.

So familiar and he has learned to love

The exquisite pain of regret.

*For all your wonderful talents,
You seem to have mastered the art
of breaking your own heart.*

Never give your heart to a wild thing, They are dangerous creatures to love.

A red lip
is a terrible thing
to waste.

She feels like the
ocean at midnight.
She smells of adventure
and single malt whiskey.

She'll lay on your chest and
read you poetry at night
wearing nothing but
your T-Shirt.

She'll have you dancing
on tables and forgetting
you never really liked
dancing anyway.

That was her magic.

She brought out the animal in me.
That primal desire she could conjure
with a flash of her eye.
She makes me more wolf than man.

These men;
Each one a different hat I try on,
A different look I entertain for a while.
Until I remember;
I was never much for hats anyway.

It's that moment, you know the one,
 where you find yourself justifying and excusing.
Renegotiating your own boundaries and standards
with yourself on their behalf.
Did they ask you?
No my darling, you see we do that all by ourselves,
like good little girls, without even being asked,

We drop standards and move boundaries,
we manoeuvre and bend like we're trying
to squeeze into those damn jeans we know won't fit.
But maybe if you just try a little harder,
move a little more, you just might fit.
I ask you; at what cost?
your happiness? your self worth? your dignity? your self respect?
Yes, all of them.
Stand Strong. stand in your light, in your power.
Stand in the beautiful qualities that brought them to you in the first place.

They will come and go, they are meant too.
They can take what they came with and maybe a memory or two
but never YOUR power,
never YOUR worth.

We are always teaching and learning in every relationship,
 the key is knowing who has the gumption to graduate,
Until then, schools out.

The truth. Authenticity.
I want it to be real.
I want it to be true.
I want to be sure.
Because I am sure,
if it's not true;
it's not real.

Be careful,
my girl,
Don't open
too much
or linger too long,
For you are
addictive you know,
and just like
that first rush,
they will forever
chase the shadow
that you are.

What a beautiful lie;
A man walking towards me,
asking for my heart.
he wears clothes too big for him,
walks in shoes that aren't his.
You're a pretender, my sweet.
A boy wishing for a Queen.
But this is not your kingdom, not your throne.
You must earn this space beside me.
You must learn this space beside me.
So roar again my little cub,
for one day you may become a lion.
We had some fun for a time,
but as the queen herself says;
I fucks with you, til I realise,
I'm just too much for you.

I still love you

I've come to learn a great many things about love,
I've changed my mind, argued with myself, questioned everything.
Though however many times I may revise my thinking,
Of this I am certain;

We must learn to love what is good for us.
It is a choice.
The choice to deem ourselves worthy.
The choice to love ourselves, without prejudice or judgement.

To purely and honestly choose love.
Choose a love that builds, that warms your bones.
A love that makes your soul smile and your heart swell.
A love that ignites when your energies collide.
Choose it everyday, because it's there, it's waiting for you.

Love yourself first,
deem youself worthy and life will follow.

And just like that, She took back what was rightfully hers; The middle of the bed.

November 9th, 2019

Fuck having a side.

Sit in the hard.
Feel yourself.
The answers are there.
It is both the illness
and the antidote.

And there it was; between the pinot and the brie on that Sunday amongst the vines; The place where love resides.

That freedom felt like
clean sheets on a Sunday;
Crisp and fresh with the
promise of new beginnings.

"I don't believe in miracles" she sighed. He leaned over and opened her window shade, "And yet here you are, flying through the sky with the clouds at your feet."

Ascension. Elevation.
It can hit you like a lightning bolt, a rush in the dark.
It can feel like falling, transcending.
It can hurt, it's confusing, frightening and isolating.
Just as it becomes too much to bear,
just as your head dips below the surface
and you take your seemingly last breath;
you are catapulted into the light,
luminescent sun warming your bones,
hope rushing through your veins.

Never forget, my darling,
it is always darkest right before the dawn.

There is nothing quite like the overheard conversations at an air airport bar to remind you that we are all vagabonds at heart.

I am never lost, just purposefully wandering,
seeking solitude, breathing in my peace.
This is where the lessons are you see,
They live in the grains of sand on the shore,
In the tide of the ocean and among the trees.
And if we only look,
Our greatest teacher, nature, shows us
no matter the circumstance, we shall always persevere.

I yearn for the unknown adventure.
Countries not yet explored, lips not yet kissed.
To hear my footseps on the streets of paris at midnight.
To feel the morning sun on my face in Budapest.
To lock eyes with a stranger
in a dark bar in Amsterdam.
To ride on the back of a scooter through
the streets of Rome.
To feel the wind on my face as I stand through
the sunroof of a jeep speeding through
the streets of Tulum.
To taste black coffee on a balcony in Venice
wearing ntohing but a mans shirt.
I yearn for the unknown adventure.

As the morning light peeked
through and danced on her cheeks,
A smile crept across her face;
it was a new day, a rebirth.
A beautiful season was calling.

*Do not shy away,
for your broken-ness is your beauty.*

If we're going to heal, let it be glorious.
If we're going to burn, let it be furious.
If we're going to rise, let it be unstoppable.
If we're going to be heard, let it be loud and damn clear.
If we're going to lift eachother up, let it be forever,
not for a day, a week, until it stops trending - let it be always.
This is for all of us, young, old, struggling or soaring.
I love you, I've got you, I am you.

*Gratitude Wins,
Always.*

*I thank you and I love you,
always, in all ways.*

x

www.ingramcontent.com/pod-product-compliance
Lightning Source LLC
Chambersburg PA
CBHW042047290426
44109CB00006B/138